The Inside Track

FORMULA 1 DRIVER

Paul Mason

EDGE FRANKLIN WATTS

LONDON·SYDNEY

Franklin Watts
First published in Great Britain in 2016 by
The Watts Publishing Group

Copyright © The Watts Publishing
Group 2016

Credits
Executive editor: Adrian Cole
Series designer: Mayer Media
Design manager: Peter Scoulding
Picture researcher: Diana Morris

Photo acknowledgements:
Eniko Balogh/Shutterstock: 1, 4t, 7b, 10b, 14bl,
29t. Charles Coates/Getty Images: 9b. Adem
Demir/Shutterstock: 21b. efecreata medigroup/
Shutterstock: 30cra. Ivan Garcia/Shutterstock:
30crb. Glebstock/Shutterstock: 6t. hxdbzxy/
Shutterstock: front cover tr. Evren Kallinbacak/
Shutterstock: 4b. kts design/Shutterstock: front
cover tl. Bryn Lennon/Getty Images: front cover t.
Fabrizio Mariani/Dreamstime: 31tl, 31cr, 31cl, 31br.
Robert Marquardt/Getty Images: 27t. Nuralya/
Dreamstime: 14br. Jaget Rashidi/Shutterstock:
5t. Vladimir Rys/Getty Images: front cover c. Z
Ryzner/Shutterstock: 6c, 10c, 13b, 22b, 23b,
24c. Jewel Samad/AFP/Getty Images: 8c. Rainer
W. Schlegelmilch/Getty Images: 16c, 18c. Oskar
Schuler/Shutterstock: 30tr. Mr Segui/Shutterstock:
20c, 26c, 30cr. Studio 1A/Shutterstock: 30br.
Mark Thompson/Getty Images: 17c, 29b. Znockz /
Dreamstime: 12b.

Every attempt has been made to
clear copyright. Should there be any
inadvertent omission please apply
to the publisher for rectification.

Dewey number 796.7'2'0922
HB ISBN 978 1 4451 4504 4
Library ebook ISBN 978 1 4451 4689 8

Printed in China

Franklin Watts
An imprint of
Hachette Children's Group
Part of The Watts Publishing Group
Carmelite House
50 Victoria Embankment
London EC4Y 0DZ

An Hachette UK Company
www.hachette.co.uk

www.franklinwatts.co.uk

*The narrative within this book is a work
of fiction and all statements purporting
to be facts are not necessarily true.*

*The statistics were correct at the time this book
was printed, but because of the nature of the sport,
it cannot be guaranteed that they are now accurate.*

*The tweets in this book have been reproduced as
they originally appeared on Twitter, and as a result
may contain inaccuracies and do not express the
views or opinions of the Publisher or Author.*

MIX
Paper from
responsible sources
FSC® C104740

FSC
www.fsc.org

CONTENTS

DRIVER BIO

NAME: Lewis Hamilton

TEAM: Mercedes

BORN: 1985 in UK (Stevenage)

Famous for his aggressive driving style and exciting overtaking, Hamilton is a driver the public loves to watch. He went into the last race of 2014 with a career total of 32 Formula 1 wins and 38 pole positions.

Lewis Hamilton's first year in Formula 1 was 2007. His team-mate was two-time world champion Fernando Alonso. Hamilton was just there to learn. At least, that's what everyone *thought*...

By the end of the year, Hamilton had beaten Alonso, and come second in the Drivers' Championship, missing out on first by just one point! The next year, 2008, Hamilton won the title.

By 2014, Hamilton was very hungry for another Drivers' Championship. By the final race, in Abu Dhabi, he had...

◉ won ten races

◉ claimed pole position seven times

◉ set the fastest lap in races seven times

There was just one thing that could stop Hamilton winning the Drivers' Championship again — his Mercedes team-mate, Nico Rosberg.

DRIVER BIO

NAME: Nico Rosberg

TEAM: Mercedes

BORN: 1985 in Germany (Wiesbaden)

Son of a former Formula 1 racer, Rosberg is brilliant at qualifying. He went into the final race of the 2014 Formula 1 season with a career total of 15 pole positions and 8 Formula 1 wins.

In Rosberg's first ever Grand Prix in 2006, he recorded the fastest lap of the race. Rosberg became the youngest driver ever to do this.

Rosberg's speed did not surprise anyone who had seen him race before. He had been a champion kart racer as a boy, and then won the GP2 World Championship in 2005. This earned him a place on the Williams Formula 1 team for 2006.

In 2014 Rosberg moved to Mercedes. He was so fast in the new car that by the last race of the year Rosberg had...

- won five races

- claimed pole position ten times

- set the fastest lap in races five times

Rosberg and Hamilton had been friends and rivals for years. Now, though, they were just rivals...both desperate to win the 2014 Drivers' Championship.

FRIDAY PRACTICE

This is the story of Lewis Hamilton's biggest race — told from the inside!

By Thursday night the Mercedes crews have put the cars together at the Yas Marina track in Abu Dhabi. They are examined and approved by the FIA inspectors. If the cars don't pass, the drivers might not be able to race!

Our cars pass the FIA inspection, so we're all set for Friday practice.

Lewis walks round the track with our #TeamLH race engineer before practice starts. He does this before every race, it's part of his pre-race routine. They talk quietly about the track, the car and the race, away from all the engine noise and press people in the pit lane.

FIA Fédération Internationale de l'Automobile the world governing body for motorsports

#TeamLH Lewis's Mercedes crew - this is the Twitter hashtag they use

pit lane area off the racing track where each team has a garage for working on the cars

There is one practice session in the morning, and another one in the afternoon. By the afternoon the temperature is *baking* hot — nearly 43 degrees Celsius. It's uncomfortable to be out in the air even if you're just standing still!

Driving in a hot race is very uncomfortable. I once heard a driver say that at the Malaysian Grand Prix, he was crying with pain during the last few laps. Most drivers finish hot races about 3kg lighter, because of the amount of fluid they sweat out.

#TeamLH use the practice sessions to work out how the car could go faster. Lewis tells us how it feels to drive and where he thinks he can get more speed. Then the engineers adjust the set up.

END OF PRACTICE RESULTS

1	Lewis **Hamilton**	Mercedes	● ● ●	1.42.113
2	Nico **Rosberg**	Mercedes	● ● ●	1.42.196
3	Kevin **Magnussen**	McLaren	● ● ●	1.42.895
4	Sebastian **Vettel**	Red Bull	● ● ●	1.42.959
5	Valtteri **Bottas**	Williams	● ● ●	1.43.070

At the end of practice Rosberg is just 0.083 seconds behind. But anyone seeing this tweet from Lewis can probably work out that he thinks there will be more to come in the race tomorrow.

@lewishamilton
It's been a good Friday!

↩   ↻ 5   ★ 5   •••

After Friday practice the engineers fine-tune Lewis's car. We run pre-qualifying computer diagnostics, and check everything multiple times before tomorrow's qualifying sessions. If the car starts the qualifying sessions performing poorly, or develops a fault, there's only a very limited amount of time for us to try to put it right before the race.

Any mistakes we make now will also make things worse later. For example, say we already know there's a problem with the suspension balance. If we have to fix something else from the pre-qualifying checks, we might not have time to fix the suspension problem. There is limited time, and a limited number of people to help.

diagnostics a system of computer checks to look for specific problems

Setting up the car for a particular track is a tricky balance to get right. The engine, tyres, suspension, aerodynamics, computer software and thousands of parts all have to work together under a great deal of stress, and for the whole race.

Fortunately, Lewis is really happy with the way the car feels:

"The car feels great - the best I've ever driven here, without doubt. The team have done an amazing job."

Seeing that on your driver's blog makes everyone a) proud, and b) determined to work even harder. If adjustments to the car are needed tomorrow, they should only be minor ones.

TEAM BIO

NAME: Paddy Lowe

TEAM: Mercedes

JOB: Executive Director (Technical)

Lowe joined Mercedes in 2013. He oversaw the development of the 2014 Mercedes F1 W05 — a car that won a total of 16 out of the 19 races in the 2014 Formula 1 season.

... but you can lose!

Even Lewis would struggle to start from the back and *win* — and winning is what we *really* want to do this weekend. To do that, we have to get the car as close to the front of the starting grid as possible. Qualifying has to be faultless.

Everyone on our side of the Mercedes garage, from the driver to the newest member of the pit crew, has to pull together to get qualifying right. Knowing that the Drivers' Championship is on the line, we have to make sure every job is done perfectly.

@lewishamilton
This is it guys. We win & lose together.

Fortunately, in this first qualifying session there are no mistakes, and no problems with the car. It's a super-cool drive by Lewis, who puts in a smooth, fast lap and finishes fastest. Rosberg is second, 0.101 of a second behind.

QUALIFYING 1 2014 ABU DHABI GRAND PRIX		
P Driver	Team	Time
1 Lewis **Hamilton**	Mercedes	1.41.207
2 Nico **Rosberg**	Mercedes	1.41.308
3 Felipe **Massa**	Williams	1.41.475
4 Kevin **Magnussen**	McLaren	1.42.104
5 Jenson **Button**	McLaren	1.42.137

Over on Rosberg's side of the Mercedes garage they're not looking at all worried. They obviously think Rosberg can go faster, but so can Lewis!

Slowest in qualifying are the usual people. These guys are all good drivers — *really* good drivers — but their teams don't have the budget to build a really fast car. Only 15 of the 20 cars go through to Q2: today, two Caterhams, two Lotuses and a Sauber are all knocked out.

budget amount of money that can be spent on something
Q2 qualifying is split into 3 phases: Q1, Q2 and Q3

After Q1 has finished, the action pauses. We spend the time analysing car and track data, and preparing to go out again. Then the cars are back on track for Q2.

When Lewis gets out on the track, he's absolutely flying! He just drove one of the best laps the circuit has ever seen. He was the only driver to break 1.41.00 for a lap of the 5.554 km circuit. That's an average speed of 198 kph!

The Williams drivers are on a charge, though. Massa went 0.331 faster than he had managed in Q1. He's only 0.224 behind Lewis, which is a bit too close for comfort. Bottas improved by an amazing 0.970 seconds! Rosberg seemed to be feeling the pressure at last. He made a mistake, locked up his brakes (below), ran wide on turn 20 and finished fourth fastest.

locked up when the brakes are applied too hard and the wheel stops turning (causing tyre wear)

QUALIFYING 2 2014 ABU DHABI GRAND PRIX			
P	Driver	Team	Time
1	Lewis **Hamilton**	Mercedes	1.40.920
2	Felipe **Massa**	Williams	1.41.144
3	Valtteri **Bottas**	Williams	1.41.376
4	Nico **Rosberg**	Mercedes	1.41.459
5	Daniel **Ricciardo**	Red Bull	1.42.692

Rosberg is actually really good at qualifying. In fact, he's the only team-mate Lewis has ever had who's out-qualified him through a whole season. If Lewis can be fastest after Q3, he should be on the front of the grid for the race.

Has Rosberg been saving himself for one last massive effort, though? We'll find out in a few minutes, when Q3 starts...

DRIVER BIO

NAME: Felipe Massa

TEAM: Williams

BORN: 1981

Second to Hamilton for the 2008 Drivers' Championship. Massa suffered a terrible injury in 2009 when a part from another car hit him in the head. He returned to racing in 2010, and moved to Williams for the 2014 season.

out-qualified finished higher in qualifying results

Q3 is the session that decides pole position. Lewis was fastest in free practice on Friday, fastest in Q1 and fastest in Q2. Things are looking good!

... But in Formula 1 it never pays to be too confident. After Q3 — just 10 minutes — things were looking distinctly NOT-so-good.

Lewis just couldn't get a good lap together. First he came on the team radio saying he could feel vibrations in his tyres. Then he locked up his wheels and skidded into the last corner. Then he missed an apex and ran wide. In the end he was faster than in Q2, but it looked scrappy. We're probably lucky to be starting ahead of Bottas tomorrow (who went even faster than he had in Q2).

Rosberg, meanwhile, did a brilliant lap. He smashed our time by half a second, then used Twitter to tell the world:

@nico_rosberg
1st step is done. hope the next will follow. What a car! Thanks for your support out there. Amazing.

apex part of a turn where a driver comes closest to the inner edge of the track

@lewishamilton
I didn't have the best of laps today, but tomorrow is when it counts

Rosberg, of course is doing and saying everything he can to put doubts in Lewis's mind:

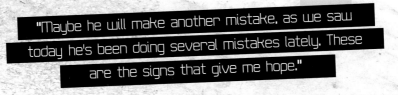

"Maybe he will make another mistake, as we saw today he's been doing several mistakes lately. These are the signs that give me hope."

Lewis was quiet after qualifying — but he soon recovered. He had a chat with his friend Pharrell Williams, who's here to play at the after-race concert, and afterwards Lewis seemed a lot more cheerful.

Even so, things could be better. Tomorrow, Lewis starts on the dirty side of the track, further from the first corner, and with two Williams cars behind him. And those Williams cars are even faster in a straight line than our Mercedes!

FINAL QUALIFYING 2014 ABU DHABI GRAND PRIX

P	Driver	Team	Time
1	Nico **Rosberg**	Mercedes	1.40.480
2	Lewis **Hamilton**	Mercedes	1.40.866
3	Valtteri **Bottas**	Williams	1.41.025
4	Felipe **Massa**	Williams	1.41.119
5	Daniel **Ricciardo**	Red Bull	1.42.267

dirty side part of track - not normally used - where dirt collects and there is less grip

@lewishamilton
Today feels like the most important day of my life. But I am calm and focused. #TeamLH lets do this! Thank you!

Most drivers relax in their hotel room on Sunday morning. Lewis often listens to music: he never travels anywhere without an MP3 player and some headphones. The playlist is pretty sure to include some Notorious B.I.G, Des'ree and a bit of Nas.

Lewis starts from second today — but he's won from further back on the grid. At the British Grand Prix in July 2013, he was shattered when he messed up Q3 and only finished sixth. He went away that night and stayed with his dad Anthony, came back on Sunday and won.

Lewis was upset yesterday after qualifying second. But like the title of the poem by Maya Angelou *Still I Rise* (which he has tattooed on his back) Lewis keeps fighting back. This morning, he looks as determined as he's ever been.

Once a driver gets to the Abu Dhabi circuit, there isn't really a spare minute. There's a drivers' parade for the crowd, talks with the engineers, discussions about strategy for the race, getting changed into a driving suit — and then suddenly there are just 30 minutes before the start. Time to get the car out on the grid!

Out there it's a crush of celebrities, engineers and TV crews looking for last-minute interviews. The drivers often disappear for a final wee (they drink a lot before a hot race like this). Then 10 minutes before the start, the grid is cleared leaving only the drivers in their cars. The car engines fire up, and the drivers set off on the formation lap.

When they get back, everyone lines up in position on the grid. The race is seconds away from starting.

This is it: the race that will decide this year's Formula 1 Drivers' Championship.

formation lap single lap before the start of a race

WHEN THE LIGHTS GO OUT

At almost every race start, *someone* has a shocker.
At this year's Italian Grand Prix it was Lewis: he went
from first to fourth before the first corner. If the same
thing happens today, it could be disastrous.

First one red light on the start board goes on. The revs
of the car engines rise to a howl. Anyone standing nearby
without ear protectors would be deafened. Then two
lights come on, three, four, five. When all the lights go
out, the cars blast away from the grid.

This time it's not Lewis but Rosberg who has a shocker.
His car doesn't go into anti-stall: he's just slow away.
The TV replays seem to show he got a bit overexcited
and span his wheels, losing grip.

Meanwhile on the other side of the grid:

"Hamilton's made a great start! A brilliant start from
Lewis Hamilton! He snatches the lead."

By the first corner Lewis is clear of the field,
out in front, in first place!

anti-stall slow engine setting triggered automatically to make sure the engine does not stop

If we're honest, no one was sure how this first lap would play out. The top 10 drivers all have to start on the tyres they used in Q2. Lewis was faster than Rosberg in Q2, which could have been a sign that Rosberg was saving his tyres for the race.

In fact, it looks like Rosberg's mistake in Q2, where he skidded, has affected his tyres. By the end of the first lap, Lewis is pulling clear and over a second ahead. That second could be crucial when DRS becomes available. DRS gives a car that's close behind a chance to catch up or overtake — but they have to be close behind, within one second of the car in front.

FIRST LAP 2014 ABU DHABI GRAND PRIX

P	Driver	Team	Gap
1	Lewis **Hamilton**	Mercedes	
2	Nico **Rosberg**	Mercedes	+1.239
3	Felipe **Massa**	Williams	+2.549
4	Jenson **Button**	McLaren	+3.337
5	Kimi **Räikkönen**	Ferrari	+3.838

DRS short for Drag Reduction System - in which the driver can open the rear wing of the car to make it go faster

PIT STOP STRATEGY

As soon as Lewis gets to the front, the team starts talking about pit stop strategy. The driver in front gets to decide when to make a pit stop — or box — so our side of the garage will be making the call.

You can lose crucial seconds in the pit stops. You can even lose the race! To get the strategy right we have to strike a balance:

◉ If Lewis stays out on old tyres, and the cars behind him change theirs, they might use the faster fresh tyres to catch up — or even overtake.

◉ If Lewis comes in early, he'll have to come in sooner on his *second* pit stop, too — which could leave him with slow, worn tyres at the end of the race.

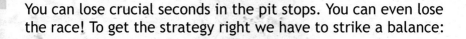

box short for 'pit box' - the area in the pit lane where a team works on the car; 'box' means 'come into the pits'

LAP 9 The first pit stop will happen soon, but we don't want Lewis to stop, change tyres, and get tangled up with another car. We wait until he'll come out on to clear track, then radio the message:

"Box, box, box."

Lewis comes out of the pits third, behind Rosberg and Massa — but they haven't yet stopped. When they do, the cars return to their original running order: Lewis, Rosberg, Massa. On lap 17 Rosberg's engineer tells him:

"The plan is simple. Keep the gap manageable to Lewis, we'll aim to go longer than him."

Lewis has to watch out. If Rosberg does make each set of tyres last longer, he will have newer, faster tyres in the last few laps. He could overtake Lewis at the very end of the race.

PIT CREW

A pit crew can be the difference between a driver winning or losing a race, as every second in the pits is a second lost on the track. A "lollipop" operator guides the car into its box, and releases it once the pit stop is finished. Jack operators lift the front and rear of the car. Three people change each wheel. While they are working, other mechanics sometimes make quick adjustments to the car setup.

ERS FEARS

Through the season, Lewis's biggest difficulty has been problems with the car. Now that he's in the lead, the whole of #TeamLH is desperately hoping his car doesn't break down.

We're all trying not to think about what happened at the Canadian Grand Prix. Then, both Mercedes cars had a problem with their ERS system. Rosberg's recovered and he managed to finish second, behind Daniel Ricciardo. Lewis ended up dropping out of the race and scoring no points.

ERS short for Energy Recovery System - recovers energy that can be used later for a "boost"

Rosberg locks up his tyres going into a corner. Blue smoke pours off them as they slide, but Rosberg manages to keep the car running without losing too much time. It's a sign that he's pushing as hard as he can. Or is there a problem with his brakes?

Later that lap, Rosberg has a radio exchange with his engineer:

> Rosberg: "I'm losing engine power."
> Engineer: "Nico, at the moment, ERS has failed."

It's the same problem as in Canada. Lewis won't like this. First, he'll be worried that his car might have the same problem. Second, he wants to win — but by beating Rosberg, not because Rosberg's car isn't working properly.

Meanwhile Massa, in third, gets a message from his engineer that Rosberg is down on power. He's suddenly like a shark that smells blood in the water! Soon he's on Rosberg's tail. Then, on lap 26, Massa manages to get past.

DRIVER BIO

NAME: Daniel Ricciardo

TEAM: Red Bull

BORN: 1989

The driver with the biggest smile in Formula 1, Ricciardo's first season with Red Bull was in 2014. He won three races, beating team-mate (and four-times World Champion) Sebastian Vettel in the Drivers' Championship.

MANAGING THE GAP

From the outside, it seems as though everything's going brilliantly. Lewis is in the lead, and his biggest rival is struggling. So why are we all gut-churningly nervous?

It's because we know that the race isn't over until you cross the finish line! Rosberg and Lewis have cars that are almost exactly the same, and both engines are three races old. If one car develops a problem, there's a chance the other one might, too.

For Lewis, the most important things are a) finish the race and b) finish in front of Rosberg. Then he will end the season as champion. We send a wireless signal to the car, reducing the engine's power and the amount of strain on it. There's a risk of losing first place — but the Championship is more important.

LAP 30 Reducing power might have been a mistake! Lewis's lap times start to really slow down. Massa is catching him by two seconds a lap! Lewis is only 8.841 seconds ahead, with 24 laps still to go. At this rate, Massa will be looking up Lewis's exhaust pipe in four or five laps' time!

Lewis does NOT want to be beaten by Massa! Lewis always, always wants to win. He gets a message from his engineer:

Engineer: "We're just reviewing whether we need to turn the car up again. You let us know."

LAP 32 Lewis comes out of the pits after changing tyres. He's right behind Rosberg (who hasn't stopped yet) — but quickly overtakes him to go second.

season part of the year in which Formula 1 races are held: in 2014 it lasted from March-November and there were 19 races

ROSBERG'S NIGHTMARE

Rosberg is the only driver who can beat Lewis to the Drivers' Championship title. All year his car has been more reliable than Lewis's. Now, though, he's having a nightmare with it.

LAP 33 Rosberg has been overtaken by Valtteri Bottas in the second Williams car, which means he's now in fourth place. He has already sent a forlorn-sounding message to his engineer:

Rosberg: "Just get me in the top six or five or whatever it is."

Engineer: "Copy that. copy that. We'll do our best."

Rosberg has realised that his car has to be nursed to the finish: he won't win the race. But if Lewis breaks down, and Rosberg comes fifth or better, Rosberg wins the Drivers' Championship.

DRIVER BIO

NAME: Valtteri Bottas

TEAM: Williams

BORN: 1989

In 2014 Bottas only finished outside the top 10 places once in the first 13 races. He finished the year fourth in the Drivers' Championship.

LAP 35

Unfortunately for Rosberg, things get worse, not better. On lap 35, his engineer tells him, "box... you have to do a manual pull-away". The car's electrical and computer systems are failing, and without them it is almost impossible to drive.

We want Lewis to win, but you have to feel sorry for Rosberg and his engineers — we're part of the same team after all. Losing a race because your car lets you down is horrible. It leaves you thinking maybe you could have done it, if only the car had kept going.

Rosberg pulls into the pits for fresh tyres, has a slow pit stop, and comes out in 7th. Three laps later, he radios his engineer desperately:

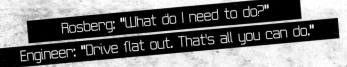

Rosberg: "What do I need to do?"

Engineer: "Drive flat out. That's all you can do."

LAP 40

Rosberg does — but it's not enough. He falls further behind, and by lap 40 he's over a minute behind Lewis. His bid to win the Drivers' Championship is over.

Now, of course, we've started to worry whether Lewis can win the race. Behind him, Massa has looked dangerous right from the start. Can Lewis hold him off?

LAP 43   Lewis puts in the fastest lap of the race and tells his engineer, "Don't turn up the car, please". So, everyone listening to race radio gets the message that he's not even at full power!

That same lap, though, Massa pulls into the pits. He comes out on supersoft, super-fast tyres, and goes on the rampage. Lewis is 10 seconds ahead — but on laps 46, 47 and 48, Massa sets the fastest times of the race.

LAP 50   With five laps to go, the gap between Lewis and Massa is just 5.5 seconds.

LAP 51   Massa is 3.750 behind...

FINAL LAP   Massa is 3.20 behind — but his tyres are cooked. Massa cannot get closer: the last lap ticks past, and Lewis finishes winner of the 2014 Abu Dhabi Grand Prix, and 2014 Drivers' Champion!

Lewis never forgets his fans, and he makes sure to send them a final message from the race weekend:

race radio radio between drivers and their engineers: their messages can be heard by officials and sometimes TV channels
cooked Formula 1 slang for tyres that are worn out

@lewishamilton
Wow! This is the greatest day of my life! Thank you everybody for all your support #bestfansintheworld

MORE TOP DRIVERS

Lewis Hamilton raced to the 2014 Drivers' Championship alongside some great drivers, whose bios are featured in this book. Here are a few more. Some are famous names from the past, others for the future.

DRIVER BIO

NAME: Ayrton Senna   **NATIONALITY:** Brazilian   **BORN:** 1960

Lewis Hamilton's hero, Senna is the driver admired by more Formula 1 drivers than any other. The official Formula 1 website says that he "drove like a man possessed". Senna won the Drivers' Championship in 1988, 1990 and 1991. He died in 1994 after crashing at the San Marino Grand Prix.

DRIVER BIO

NAME: Sebastian Vettel   **NATIONALITY:** German   **BORN:** 1987

The youngest-ever World Champion at 23 (in 2010); the youngest double World Champion (in 2011); the youngest triple and quadruple World Champion (in 2012 and 2013). Vettel left Red Bull for Ferrari - the team he had dreamed of driving for since he was a boy - at the end of the 2014 season.

DRIVER BIO

NAME: Kimi Räikkönen   **NATIONALITY:** Finnish   **BORN:** 1979

Nicknamed "The Iceman" because he hardly ever shows emotion. Räikkönen was World Champion in 2007. He is one of the fastest drivers in Formula 1 over a single lap. Räikkönen actually retired in 2009 — but came back to the sport two years later as fast as ever.

DRIVER BIO

NAME: Max Verstappen   **NATIONALITY:** Dutch   **BORN:** 1997

Verstappen's team - Torro Rosso - think he could one day be as good as the great Ayrton Senna. He became the youngest Grand Prix racer ever at the Australian Grand Prix in 2015 at just 17 years old. Then a few weeks later he became the youngest ever points scorer in Formula 1 history.

DRIVER BIO

NAME: Michael Schumacher   **NATIONALITY:** German   **BORN:** 1969

Schumacher is simply the most successful racing driver ever. He won the Drivers' Championship in 1994, 1995, 2000, 2001, 2002, 2003 and 2004. Schumacher won more races, more pole positions and more fastest laps than any driver before him.

FAMOUS RACETRACKS

Formula 1 races are held in Asia, Australia, Europe, the Middle East, and North and South America. Some racetracks, though, are special to the fans and the drivers:

MONACO GRAND PRIX, MONTE CARLO

This is an old-fashioned street-racing circuit, with sections of the track called Casino Square, Tabac (French for "newsagent") and Swimming Pool. Winning at Monaco guarantees a driver a place among the greats. The competition is especially fierce because many of the drivers live in Monaco, so they know the streets extremely well.
WATCH OUT FOR: every bend is a classic! But the tight corner at Fairmont and the downhill sweeper at Mirabeau are two of the best.

BRITISH GRAND PRIX, SILVERSTONE

A former Second World War air base, Silverstone was first used as a racing circuit in 1948. This makes it one of the oldest racetracks in Formula 1: in fact, when F1 held its first-ever race in 1950, the race was held at Silverstone.
WATCH OUT FOR: the Maggotts-Becketts-Chapel sequence of bends, a tricky left-right-left-right-left set of turns.

BELGIAN GRAND PRIX, SPA-FRANCORCHAMPS

Even older than Silverstone (the first top-level races were held here in 1924), Spa is a favourite with drivers and fans. The track is narrow and long, and winds up and down through the wooded hills of Belgium. It is notoriously difficult to drive well.
WATCH OUT FOR: the incredible Eau Rouge section, where the track crosses a stream before sweeping left, then right, then left again over a blind summit.

ITALIAN GRAND PRIX, MONZA

Built in 1922, Monza is a circuit where the ghosts of old drivers drift among the trees beside the track. Known as "the temple of speed", Monza is as famous for terrible accidents as for its exciting races.
WATCH OUT FOR: the Parabolica, a long, long right-hand turn where the track turns through 180 degrees before arriving at the start-finish straight. High exit speed is crucial if you want to overtake.

blind summit top of an uphill section where the rest of the track cannot be seen

GLOSSARY & INDEX

GLOSSARY

aerodynamics — Having a shape that reduces the drag from air moving past a solid object, such as a car.

circuit — The loop round which each car repeatedly travels during a race.

Drivers' Championship — A series of races held during a year to determine the fastest and most successful racing car driver.

ear protectors — Special headphones worn to prevent loud noises damaging ears.

Formula 1 — The top level of professional track car motorsport.

Grand Prix — The name given to each individual race within the Formula One World Drivers' Championship.

grid — A marked-out area of the track where the racing cars line up to start the race.

qualifying — To be good enough to go to the final round of a competition by reaching a certain standard or beating other competitors.

strategy — A plan of action to achieve a particular goal or aim.

suspension — The system of springs and shock absorbers that supports a car on its wheels.

vibrations — Rapid movement to and fro.

INDEX